ABSU AND ITS STRUGGLE FOR BODOLAND

SAHADEV SAHA

This book is dedicated to my late **mother**,

who has been the main source of inspiration for me.

Contents

Foreword

ABSU its struggle for BODOLAND

This book mainly discusses the long struggle of ABSU in Bodoland movement. ABSU as a non-political students organization contributed a lot to make this movement a mass movement. As this movement is an ongoing movement ABSU is still playing a leading role to make their long pending demand of separate state within India.

ABSU its struggle for BODOLAND

Preface

This book is a result of my self-research. The book is entitled as **"ABSU and its struggle for Bodoland "**. I am fortunate enough that I have closely experienced few activities of this movement led by ABSU. I will be very grateful if this book serves academic needs of the Students.

Acknowledgements

I am grateful to the Notionpress for giving me opportunity to prepare and publish this book and believing in me. At the same time I would also grateful to my publisher representative. I offer my gratitude to all my well wishers, my family and friends for their encouragement and inspiration.

Last but not at the least I am thankful to my friend Sudeep Mandal for his constant guidance and co-operation.

CHAPTER ONE

Introduction

All Bodo Student Union (ABSU) is a Student organization, (non-political) formed on February 15, 1967, in the Bodoland region of Assam. ABSU was formed at a meeting held at Kokrajhar Tribal Rest House. Baneswar Basumatary and Kankeswar Narzary (khungra) were elected as President and General Secretary.

ABSU is the organization of all Bodo students and youth covering the jurisdiction wherever the Bodos are found around the world and as such it has been nomenclature as the All Bodo Students Union (ABSU). That is why the organization is not called All Assam Bodo Students Union (AABSU) which should have comprised only Assam. Presently, the All Bodo Students Union (ABSU) comprises the Bodo student's community of Assam, Meghalaya, West-Bangal, Nepal, and Nagaland have representative from these state.

The prime objectives of ABSU were to unite the Bodos for the presentation of their rich cultural heritage As embodied in the constitution of ABSU that the Union shall try to achieve better mutual understanding among the Bodo students and public of different parts of India and abroad, the union shall make effort to find out ways and means to propagate among the masses, the need to imparting education through mother tongue, improve the Bodo language through publication of magazines and other literary works. It also aims to develop and safeguard the culture of the Bodos by bringing reforms to it through various perspectives, to develop the boo race economically by taking economic programmers from time to time and to settle the issues relating to the political crisis that may arise among the plains tribal people threatening the national existence of their future generation. Though the ABSU is a socio-economic, literary and cultural organization it struggle to achieve the just and constitutional rights through democratic process and fight for all round security. If the above goals are denied and ignored, the union shall not refrain even from struggling for political self-determination within the framework of Indian constitution. Further, the ABSU will support the principle of socialism for economic emancipation, raise voice for the human right and civil liberties. The ABSU shall also work for the development of socio-cultural relations among the various groups of Bodo nationality living around the world and work for the all-round prosperity of the Bodos to extent of advance nationalities of the world. Initially ABSU paid more attention to the development of Bodo society but for various social and political reason the organization had to associate itself with different movements.[1]

The Bodoland movement is an autonomy movement and movement for separate state under the jurisdiction of India. The official Bodoland movement start on 2nd of March 1987 under the leadership of Upendranath Brahma of All Bodo Students Union (ABSU). ABSU as one of the

[1] . Khema Sonowal, *Why Bodo movement*,(Guwahati, EBH Publication,2013),51-52

non-political organization playing a vital role in Bodoland movement. The Bodoland movement is the most stringent tribal movement in contemporary Assam, the Bodo movement drawn its source from the feeling of discrimination, deprivation and injustice experienced by the Bodo community.

Ethnicity and identity have been the key issues of mobilization in all North East India. The Bodo movement has its origin since the colonial period. The issue of land alienation, marginalization faced from the mainstream and dominant community and the prolonged social and economic backwardness due to the step-motherly treatment of the state has been the main driving factor of the Bodoland movement.

The Growing consciousness among the bodos led to the rise of demand for separate homeland in Assam. ABSU and other organization of bodos become aware that without political resolution their cultural identities can no longer be sustained and hence they need to fight for the protection of their own identity. The encroachment upon the tribal within the Tribal Belt and Blocks after the independence disturbed the plain tribes of Assam,

Hence Bodos formed several organization, and ABSU is one of them .ABSU was founded on the 15th February 1967 at kokrajhar Tribal Rest House. Under the leadership of the ABSU a movement for separate state was launched on 2 March 1987 with demand for a separate state for the Bodos called BODOLAND. ABSU also demanded power to conserve their language, culture, customs, and protection from political domination of non-tribals.

So the Bodoland movement for a separate state for Bodos has its origins in the economic and socio-cultural aspiration of Bodo people. The general feeling of Bodos is that of neglect, exploitation, alienation and discrimination for decades is result of ABSU;s Bodoland movement.

○　: Why this Movement?

ABSU has significant role in bodoland movement. In this book reader will get the answer that why the Bodoland movement has started and why the problems of bodos have not solved till now. At contemporary time Bodoland movement is one of the most discuss issue of politics of Assam. As we know ABSU as a non- political organization has a main role in the materialization of Bodoland movement, so it is similarly significant to study the role of ABSU in Bodoland movement. Though the Bodoland movement is an ongoing movement so another significant of the study is to study the present status of the Bodoland movement.

: Views of eminent authors regarding ABSU's stuggle in Bodo movement:

Many scholars, organization have done research on "Bodo movement" from these existing work, we got a base to go ahead in the pursuit of understanding the role of ABSU in Bodoland movement.

- **Khema Sonowal** in her work, **"why Bodo movement?"** discuss about the role of ABSU in Bodo movement and mention that ABSU is one of the most important organization among the Bodos, which remained a frontrunner in all agitation movement undertaken by the Bodos. He stated that tough the ABSU is a socio-economic, literary and cultural organization, it through Bodo movement struggles to achieve the just and constitutional rights through democratic process and fight for all round security. It also struggling for political self-determination within the framework of Indian constitution. Thus it seems that, the ABSU one of the major organization of the Bodo society, who has been working relentlessly to organize the young generations of the Bodo people. ABSU have mobilized the young generation through their well-organized network of hierarchical units. According to her, ABSU has been trying to make the young generation identity conscious and has motivated them to fight for their rights and privileges.

- **P.C Dutta** in his work **"autonomy movements in Assam"** (documents) has mention about the following role of ABSU in Bodo movement.Dutta mention that ABSU took the pioneering role and initiative along with the Bodo Sahitya Sabha in introducing Bodo medium of institution in primary level in 1963, and in 1968 for the secondary level. He also mention that ABSU played a very important role along with Bodo Sahitya Sabha for the adoption of roman script for Bodo language. He mention that ABSU has an important role in the political unification. ABSU tried it's best to unify the split of political parties of plain tribals such as the PTCA and PTCA (progressive) for launching a concerted movement for separate state.

- **Topu Choudhury** in his research journal **"Bodoland Movement: a study "**Also discuss about the following role of ABSU in Bodo movement. He mention that ABSU created a political organization the Bodo Peoples Action Committee, (BPAC) and began the Bodo movement with the slogan "divide Assam 50-50. ABSU was able to mobilize whole Bodo mass and section of other plain tribal organization in the state towards the demand of a separate state carving out of Assam. ABSU under the leadership of U.N Brahma submitted a memorandum to then Prime Minister Rajiv Gandhi.

- **M. S. Rumi Roy** in her Article **"Identity and Indigenous assertion: politics of homeland and secession in Bodoland, Assam"**, published in "JONER", 2017, edited by Dr. Jyotiraj Pathak stated that 'The Bodo movement was a significant movement in the history of Assam politics. The significant oh the Assam Accord generated the perceived feeling of being marginalized against the greater Assamese nationality among the Bodos. ABSU leader naturally took it as complete negation of composite and diverse culture and linguistic milieu of Assam. The Bodos under the banner of ABSU spearheaded a "Mass Revolution" for a separate homeland and full-fledged state for the plain Bodos and incorporated in their first memorandum.

- **Chandra Jyoti Sonowal** in his Article **"Ethnicity and ethnic conflicts in North East India- with special reference to Assam"**, published in the book "Tribal Studies in North East India", Edited by Srthak Sengupta stated that, the intensive Bodo movement found its ground, at least in the leadership level, during the Assam movement by All Assam Student Union (AASU) and All Assam Gana Sangram Parishad (AAGSP). Its learnt that the tribal leadership did not find proper place in the state issues and the movement was dominated by the caste Hindu Leadership. After forming a regional govt in the state. The demand for separate state for all tribal people of the state lost its ground and the Bodo peoples demand came to the fore. Later on, with the leadership of Upendranath Brahma the Bodoland movement got momentum under the banner of ABSU.
- **Sanjib Baruah** in his work **"India against itself, Assam and its politics of nationality"**,1999, stated that it was only in 1987, during the first Agp Government, that younger Bodo leaders begab successfully to mobilize large number of Bodos in support of a demand for a separate state to be called "BODOLAND". The most important of the organization campaigning for Bodoland i.e ABSU submitted the 92 point charter, which lists the Bodo grievances.
- **Hiar Charan Narjinari** in his work **"The saga of the Bodos"**, stated that demand for Udayanchal never materialized, due to persistent apathy of successive governments towards Bodo community. According to him in the late 1980s All Bodo student Union (ABSU) became very concerned about decades of neglect and apathy by the subsequent state government the Bodo community. ABSU with other Bodo organization jointly started a massive movement demanding a separate state called BODOLAND.

- **Ionee Basumatary**, in her work **"Politics in North East India"** stated that Bodos are demanding their separate homeland in Assam. The Bodos became aware that without political resolution, their socio cultural identity can no longer be sustained and hence they need political autonomy.

- **Jaiklong Basumatary**, in his work **"Quest for peace in Assam: A study of the Bodoland movement"** stated that the initial phase of Bodoland movement was marked by bandhs, road and rail blockades and mass mobilization effort. But it did not take long for the ABSU- led struggle to deviate from peaceful forms of protest. Even since the movement intensified, the ABSU leadership formally disowned the violent acts but did not hesitate to declare that if necessary, they would even seek foreign help to achieve their goal of separate Bodoland. He also stated that the bodo People's Action Committee (BPAC) whose formation in 1988 is considered an important landmark in the history of the Bodoland movement, was accused of adopting militant practices in its efforts to mobilize the Bodo

people. Not only it was labelled as the armed wing of ABSU but the BPAC was alas accused of adopting terrorist methods against perceived spoilers of the movement within the Bodo community and against non-bodos living in the mixed population of Dhubri, Kokrajhar, Barpeta, Nalbari, Darrang and Sonitpur district. When ABSU emerge as a force to reckon with by 1988, a marked feature of their violence had been the attacks on PTCA supporters. The ABSO-PTCA clashes not only placed the two major Bodo organization on an irreconcilable path but also led to the emergence of a fratricidal element in the Bodo agitation, resulting in the division of the Bodo people on the question of Bodoland and its equation with Assam.

- **Amites Mukhopadhyay**, in his work **"Social Movement in India"** stated that Bodo movement is also a part of social movement as well as tribal movement. The ABSU creat a political oraganisation called the Bodo Peopoles Action Committee (BPCA). The movement of ABSU began with the slogan "Divide Assam Fifty-Fifty". This movement ended up with the creation of Bodo Accord in 1993.

From above literate reviews, we can get a clear conception about the role of ABSU in Bodoland movement. ABSU as a non-political organization played a very satisfactory role in Bodoland movement but even then there is a enough scope to study the role of ABSU in Bodoland movement in a contemporary perspectives because this particular movement is an on-going movement.

AN OVER VIEW OF ABSU

◦ A BRIEF HISTORY OF ABSU:

The necessity of an all India level Bodo Students Union was felt during the first annual conference of the Goalpara District Bodo Students Union. But due to non-arrival of student representatives from south Goalpara, no discussion could be made. Accordingly, two office bearers of the Goalpara District Bodo Students Union such as Lahendra Basumatary, President and Ranjit Kumar Borgoyari, Vice-President visited Goalpara on 9th June, 1967 and met Tarun Chandra Basumatary, a student leader of south Goalpara Kanakeswar Narzary also accompanied them.

The General Secretary of Goalpara District Bodo Students Union was given the responsibility for convening a meeting for the formation of All Bodo Students Union during the first annual conference. Surath Narzary was the General Secretary at that time time. But due to unavoidable reasons, he could not convene the meeting. Ha had convened the meeting only on 31st January 1968. But as the 2nd annual conference of the Goalpara Bodo Students Union was very nearby, the meeting was cancelled.

The second annual conference, of Goalpara District Bodo students union was held on 2nd, 3rd and 4th February 1968 at Bijni Barabazar High School. Subhas Basmatari was elected as new General Secretary during the session.

After the second annual conference, Subhas Basumatari the newly elected General secretary of the Goalpara District Boro Students Union convened a meeting to discussed the matter relating to the formation of an All Boro Students Union at Kokrajhar Tribal Rest House on 15'February1968, But due to the arrival of large number of students the meeting was shifted to Kokrajhar College and was and held in a huge hall. The meeting was presided over the Phanindra Brahma. During the meeting the All Bodo Students Union was formed.

Beside student from Goalpara District the following prominent Student leaders from other District also attended the meeting:

1. New Jalpaiguri : Haricharan Narzary

1. Mahakalguri : Kiran Chandra Narzary

3. Koyrabri : Nripendra Narayan Karzi

4. Karbai Anglong : Lobindra Basumatari

5. Kamrup : Baneswar Basumatari

6. Darang : Doleswar Boro

The following members were elected office bearer of the All Bodo Students Union:

1. Baneswar Basumatari, President (Kampur).

2. Hiracharan Narzary, Vice-President (New Jalpaiguri)

3. Subhas Basumatary, Vice-President (Goalpara)

4. Kanakeswar Narzary,General Secretary (Goalpara)

5. Doleswar Boro, Joint secretary (Darrang)

6. Lobindra Basumatary, joint secretary (Karbianglong)

7. Kiran Chandra Narzary, Joint secretary (Mahakalguri)

8. Prashanta Kumar Brahma, Treasurer (Goalpara)

9. Rabindra Narzary, Joint Treasurer (New Jolpaiguri)

10. Dambarudhar Brahma, Literary Secretary (Goalpara)

11.   Arup Gwar Basumatary, Speaker (Goalpara).

The All Bodo Students Union was formed with several objectives. These objectives are:

1.   To bring unity among the Bodos

2.   To protect the political rights of the the Bodos

3.   To protect the art and culture of the Bodos

4.   To develop language and literate of the Bodos

5.   To stop exploitation by other communities

After the formation of All Bodo Students Union, necessity for written a constitution for the student union was felt. Accordingly with the responsibility of preparing draft constitution. He made the draft constitution which was later on revised under the chairmanship of Ranjit Kumar Borgoyari and accepted as the constitution of the new union.

We have discussed about the history of Bodo students Union. Thus it is observed that the Students Unions were formed with the sole objective of bringing unity among the Bodo Students. Along with it was also, formed to demand social, political and economic rights for the community in the days to come.

The following are the presidents and General Secretaries of ABSU during 1968-2003

President General Secretary

1st Baneswar Basumatary Kanakeswar Narzary

Period

1968-1972

2nd Dambarudhar Brahma Rajendra Nath Brahma

1972-1974

3rd Abhiram Boro Gobinda Basumatary

1974-1976

4th Gobinda Basumatary Premsing Brahma

1976-1979

5th Sontola Basumatary Parameswar Brahma

1979-1981

6th Dipak Kumar Baumatary Rajen Khaklary

1981-1983

7th Karendra Basumatary S.K. Bwiswmuthiary

1983-1986

8th Upendra Nath Brahma Rabiram Brahhma

1986-1990

9th Mr. S.K. Bwiswmuthairy Mr. Rabiram Brahma

1990-1993

10th Garla Batha Basumatary Maheshwar Basumatary

1993-1995

11th Swmbla Basumatary Mr. Emanuel Mushahary

1995-1996

Mr.Wrkhao Gwra Brahma Mr. Emanuel Mushahary

1996-1997

12th Mr. Wrkhao Gwra Brahma Mr. Nathuram Boro

1997-1999

13th Mr. Wrkhao Gwra Brahma Mr.Nathuram Boro

1999-2001

14th Mr. Rabiram narzary Mr. Lwmsrao Dwimary

2001-2002

15th Mr. Rabiram Narzary Mr. Rwng Gwra Brahma

2002-2003

This is a brief history of Bodo Student Union till the formation of All Bodo Students Union (ABSU) on 15th February 1968. Thus it is observed that the students union were formed with the sole objectives of bringing unity among the Bodos.

∘ : ORGANIZATIONAL STRUCTURE OF ABSU:

ABSU as a student organization work in very organize way, the members and the office bearers of the Union work in accordance with the provision mention in the constitution of the Union.

CHAPTER-II

Chapter ii of the constitution of ABSU mention about the aims and objectives of the ABSU and the organization works to achieve these aim.

AIMS AND OBJECTIVES

3. The main aims and objectives of the ABSU is to promote language, literature and culture of the Bodos. Bodo students and people of different parts of India and abroad. The Union shall make efforts, particularly to find out ways and means to:

    a. Propagate the education through the mother tongue (Bodo language) among the masses.
    b. Improve and develop the Bodo language and literature through various literary activities, publication works etc.
    c. Work for the welfare and development of the student's community in the educational field.

    d. Safeguard and develop the culture of the Bodos.

    e. Develop the Bodo nation economically by taking economic agenda and programmers time to time.

    f. Tackle and settle the political issues if and when the existence of the Bodos people is threatened, though the ABSU is a non-political organization.
    g. Struggle to achieve the rights and privileges given in the Indian Constitution through democratic process.
    h. Support the principle of democratic socialism for economic emancipation. But the Union shall welcome the principles of new economic order that may emerge from time to time.
    a. Fight for ensuring safety & security, dignity & securing Human Rights and Civil Life style of the Bodo Nationality living around the world.

CHAPTER-III

Chapter iii of the constitution of ABSU clearly discuss about the provision relating to the construction of the Organization.

CONSTITUTION

4. ABSU shall run with 4(four) main organization levels:

   a. Central Committee, ABSU (C.C., ABSU)

   b. State Committee, ABSU (S.C., ABSU)

   c. District Committee, ABSU (D.C., ABSU)

   d. Anchalik Committee, ABSU (A.C., ABSU)

5. The C.C., ABSU shall be constituted with the members selected from different S.C., D .C., ABSU in every terminating conference.
6. The jurisdiction of the Union shall be all over India and abroad.

7. A.D.C., ABSU shall be constituted within a Sub-Division of a geo-political district or within a geo-political district itself. Nevertheless, there shall not be:

 i. More than three such D.C.s within a geopolitical district or

 ii. More than ten executive Members from S.C/ D.C.s to the C.C., Ten Executive Members from to the D.C. to the S.C., Five executive Members from A.C. to the D.C. and three Executive members for Schools, Colleges, Universities and Unit Committee to A.C.
iii. In some Metropolitan cities and Universities where S.C or D.C is not existent, ABSU committee of the status of District committee can be formed. This type of committee shall have direct representation to the C.C and from such committee only five executive members shall be taken in the C.C.

7. (A) A.S.C., ABSU shall be constituted with the members selected from different district committees. However, the Central committee, ABSU, shall have the power to decide upon the matters pertaining to any controversy involving the formation of the S.C & D.C. ABSU Committees

with the special district committee status.

8. An A.C., ABSU shall be formed in certain areas or towns as per the convenience for organization of the D.C., ABSU concerned.

Such an A.C. may form a Union for the convenience of organization, some units in an educational institution such as a Universities, College or High School or even in a village falling under the jurisdiction of that A.C.

9. The representation or official correspondence among different organizational levels shall be form a lower level to the next higher level or vice-versa. As such an A.C., ABSU shall not be entitled to make any direct representation or correspondence to the C.C., ABSU.

A.C., ABSU shall solely be responsible for collection of general membership of the ABSU or of receiving institution from the D.C., ABSU concerned.

CHAPTER-I V

Chapter iv of the constitution of discuss about the provision relating to the membership of the organization:

MEMBERSHIP

10. Students who are in obligation of the principles of the ABSU shall be its members.

10. (A). Executive members and office bearers shall have to take an oath of office secrecy to carry on their responsibilities and express allegiance to the constitution,

The newly elected president shall be sworn in by the care-taker president selected on the occasion of new Body formation and other members and office bearers' oath taking ceremony shall be conducted by the new president in a meeting of charge hand over/take over.

11. Persons who have enrolled in any educational institution or leaving of the educational institution is not exceeded more than five years and has still interested in the organization shall be entitled to became a member of the ABSU.

    Students having membership in other organization whose ideas and objects are not in conformity with those of the ABSU shall not be entitled for membership in the ABSU.

12. Students having no previous records of being General member of the ABSU shall not be eligible for membership in the C.C., ABSU. For such purpose, I. Card shall be issued and registration for General Members shall be maintained.

13. Every General Member shall require to pay Rs. 20.00(Rupees Twenty) as an Annual General Membership fee.

14. Subject to section 60. (A). Two-Thirds of the fees collected by an A.C.,ABSU under section 13 of chapter-IV shall go to D.C. concerned, 60% of D.C.'s share shall go the S.C. and 40% of S.C.'s share shall go to the C.C.,ABSU.

15. The annual Executive Membership fee for C.C., S.C., D.C. and A.C. ABSU shall be of the rate of Rs. 30.00 (Rupees Thirty) only each.

16. The membership of any student shall cease to be valid if he/she fails to pay the annual membership fee of the prescribed rate. This is applicable to the members of all the organization levels of the Union excepting the members of the cabinet of the ABSU.

17. A single member shall not be an office bearer in both C.C., ABSU and D.C., ABSU or S.C., ABSU or in both D.C.,

    ABSU and A.C., ABSU or in both C.C., ABSU and an A.C., ABSU.

CHAPTER-V

CENTRAL COMMITTEE/ABSU

Chapter v of the constitution of ABSU discus about the Central committee of ABSU:

18. The C.C./ABSU shall consist of two bodies viz.-

 i. Central Working Committee/ABSU (C.W.C./ABSU) and

 ii. Cabinet of the ABSU (C.A.B.S.U)

19. The CWC/ABSU shall consist of all the executive members selected or elected as per section

 7. Clause 7 (ii), Sub-section 7.A. of the C.C.ABSU and the ex-officio members from S.C.,D.C,/ABSU.

20. CABSU shall consist of all the portfolio holding members from the C.C./ABSU.

21. In CABSU, there shall be following office bearers: Central Committee, ABSU (Cabinet):

 1. One President

 2. Two vice-President (V.P)

 3. One General Secretary (G.S)

 4. One Assistant General Secretary, Four Secretaries

 5. One Speaker

 6. One Deputy Speaker

 7. Four Secretaries, Public Relation

 8. One Cultural Secretary

 9. One Assistant Cultural Secretary

 10. One Literary Secretary

 11. One Assistant Literary secretary

12.   One sports Secretary

13.   One assistant Sports Secretary

14.   One Debating Secretary

15.   One Treasurer

16.   One Education Secretary

17.   One Assistant Education Secretary

18.   Two Advisers, preferably to select the immediately outgoing
      President And General Secretary.

In case of formation of S.C., D.C. and A.C. also the same portfolios shall
be followed and in case of A.C. one more portfolio shall be added-i.e.- One
Social Service secretary.

21.(A). The State Committee, ABSU (S.C./ABSU), shall consist of the
portfolios as in the section 21.

22.   The term of the C.C/ABSU, S.C./ABSU,D.C./ABSU and A.C./ABSU shall
      be of two years provided that a new C.C./ABSU, S.C./ABSU D.C./ABSU
      and A.C./ABSU is formed in their terminating conferences.

If a terminating conference fails to be held in due date for certain
unavoidable circumstances the C.C./ABSU, S.C./ABSU,D.C./ABSU and
A.C./ABSU may be given extension to function for a period of six months
through a resolution by the CWC of respective ABSU levels.

23.   If any vacancy occurs due to death, resignation or dismissal for
      impeachment during the term of CABSU, the same shall be filled up by
      the CWC/ABSU by selecting member from within.
24.   CABSU shall sit at least three times in a year. One Third of its members
      shall make its quorum.
25.   The CWC/ABSU shall sit six times at the minimum in a year. The
      absolute majority of it shall make the quorum.

26. If the CWC/ABSU fails to make quorum two times consecutively the president by exercising his/her discretionary power shall allow the sitting to run.

27. Any bill passed in CABSU shall be placed in the sitting of CWC/ABSU for its final approval.

Provided that CWC/ABSU fails to decide any bill due to controversies among the members, the bill shall lay at the disposal of CABSU for final decision. This shall hold good only in general cases. In organizational disputes the decision of the C.C.ABSU shall, however, be final.

CHAPTER-VI

DISTRICT COMMITTEE/ABSU

Chapter vi of the constitution of ABSU discuss about organizational structure of the District Committee of ABSU:

28. A.D.C/ABSU shall be formed under section 7 of chapter III taking at least one member from each A.C. under its jurisdiction.

29. In the DWC/ABSU there shall be the following office bearers.

    1. 1. One President

    2. Two vice-President (V.P)

    3. One General Secretary (G.S)

    4. One Assistant General Secretary, Four Secretaries

    5. One Speaker

    6. One Deputy Speaker

    7. Four Secretaries, Public Relation

    8. One Cultural Secretary

    9. One Assistant Cultural Secretary

10. One Literary Secretary

11. One Assistant Literary secretary

12. One sports Secretary

13. One assistant Sports Secretary

14. One Debating Secretary

15. One Treasurer

16. One Education Secretary

17. One Assistant Education Secretary

18. Two Advisers, preferably to select the immediately outgoing President And General Secretary.

30. The term of D.C./ABSU shall be as provided under section 22 of Chapter-V as in the case of the C.C./ABSU.
31. A new DWC/ABSU shall be constituted as provided under section 5 of Chapter-III as in the case of C.C./ABSU.
32. Vacancies of any portfolios shall be filled up as per the provision provided under section 23 of Chapter-V as in the case of the C.C./ABSU.
33. Sitting of the DWC/ABSU shall be convened as per the provision provided under section 25 of Chapter-V as in the case of the C.C./ABSU.

Any resolution (s) passed in the DWC/ABSU meeting shall be communicated to the CWC/ABSU.

34. Quorum of the DWC/ABSU shall be formed under section 25 Chapter-V.

35. For any vital issue of great consequence the D.C./ABSU shall make due consultation with the C.C./ABSU prior to taking any decision in that

regard.

CHAPTER-VII

Chapter vii of the constitution of ABSU discuss about the Anchalik Committee of ABSU:

ANCHALIK COMMITTEE/ABBSU

36. An A.C./ABSU shall be constituted as per the provision under Section 8 & Chapter-III.

37. An A.C./ABSU shall constituted in the similar way as provided under Section 7 of Chapter- III.

38. In the AWC. /ABSU there shall be portfolios as per the provision provided under Section 29 Chapter-VI.

39. An AWC/ ABSU shall sit as may times as many times as required but not less than nine times in a year.

40. Any resolution (s) passed in the meeting of an A.C/ABSU shall be communicated to its respective DC/ABSU.

41. Two-Thirds of the total members of an AWC/ABSU shall make the quorum.

42. Any vacancy of Office bearer to an AC/ABSU shall be filled up by it from among its Executive Members.

43. The term of an AC/ABSU shall be as provided under Section 22 of Chapter-V provided that a new A.C./ABSU be formed under section 8 Chapter-III.

CHAPTER-VIII

Chapter viii of the constitution of ABSU discuss about the power and function of the president and office bearers of the Union:

POWER AND FUNCTION OF THE OFFICE BEARERS

44. The President.

The President of the A.C./ABSU shall be the 'Head of the Union'.

i. The president shall preside over all the meetings of the C.C./ABSU and the CWC/ABSU.

ii. He /She shall be responsible for maintenance of discipline in the meeting.

iii. Under any circumstances, if the General Secretary remains inactive, the president shall direct the Assistant General Secretary or any one Secretary to carry out the function of the General Secretary.

iv. Under any circumstances, if both the speakers remain inactive, the president shall direct the General Secretary to convene the meeting.

v. If any of the members of CABSU remains inactive the President shall entrust a suitable member from the CWC/ABSU to hold the office after receiving due approval of the CWC/ABSU.

vi. The president shall preside over the open meeting held on the occasion of the conference of the Union.

He/she shall be entitled to present the Presidential address in a written/ printed from in the same after receiving due approval of the CWC/ABSU.

vii. On certain burning problem of common interest or of interest concerning the Union, he/she alone or jointly with the General Secretary shall issue a press statement.

viii. If a DC/ABSU goes out of the binding of the Union, the president shall exercise discretionary power to put such a DC/ABSU in dissolution after receiving due approval of the CWC/ABSU.

ix. If any remember of the CWC/ABSU involves in anti-organization activities and supporting proofs are available confirming the same, The President shall have the power to expel/suspend him/her for three consecutive years on the advice of the CWC/ABSU.

x. The President shall have a personal Emergency Fund to meet emergent expenses.

xi. The President shall have the power to dissolve the Central Executive Body (C.E.B) in the terminating Annual Conference so as to enable the organization to from a new C.E.B. and the declaration of dissolution shall be as per the form given in the Annexure-II

45. The Vice-President.

i. In absence of the President, any one of the two Vice-Presidents entrusted by the General Secretary shall preside over the meeting.

ii. On occurrence of vacancy due to death, resignation or dismissal for impeachment to the President, the CWC/ABSU shall choose either of the two Vice-Presidents for the post of the President.

46. The General Secretary.

i. The General Secretary shall mainly be responsible for any or all of the activities of the Union .For adoption of policy or in setting difficult problems, he/she shall consult with the president and such a policy or a problem may be placed in the CWC/ABSU as and when deemed necessary by him/her.

ii. He/ She shall maintain all the accounts of the Union.

iii. The annual report on the activities of the Union prepared by him/her for presenting on the occasion of the annual conference of the Union shall have to be approved by the CWC/ABSU and delegates' sitting.

iv. On certain burning problems of common interest or of interest concerning the Union, he/she alone or jointly with the President shall issue a press statement.

v. He/she shall direct the Assistant General Secretary or any one of the Secretaries to carry out activities of any kind, as and when he/she feels necessary.

47. The Assistant General Secretary and Secretaries.

i. In absence of the General Secretary, The Assistant General Secretary or one of the Secretaries, as directed by the president, shall function as the General Secretary.

ii. The provisions of section 45, sub-section-ii) shall be enjoyed by the Assistant General Secretary or the secretaries as in the case of 'President' and Vice-President", being substituted by the terms 'General Secretary' respectively.

48. The Speaker

i. The Speaker shall convene the meeting of the CWC/ABSU and CABSU as and when directed by the General Secretary.

ii. He/ She shall preside over the delegates sitting held on the occasion of the conference of the Union. In which he/she shall mainly be responsible for maintaining discipline.

49. The Deputy Speaker

i) In absence of the Speaker, The Deputy Speaker shall discharge the duties of the Speaker.

50. The Secretaries, public relation.

i. The public relation Secretaries shall look after the organizational matters of the union respectively.

ii. They shall try to make the Union popular among the masses for convenience; they may divide the jurisdiction of the union into two organizational Zones.

51. The Cultural Secretary.

i. The Cultural Secretary shall convene cultural meets from time to time in consultation with the CWC/ABSU so as to develop the Bodo culture.

ii. The Cultural Secretary shall conduct the cultural competitions held on the occasion of the conference of ABSU.

52. The Assistant Cultural Secretary

i. The Assistant Cultural Secretary shall discharge the duties of the Cultural Secretary in absence of the latter.

ii. He/ She shall help the Cultural Secretary by all means during the cultural meets and competition.

53. The Literary Secretary.

i. The Literary Secretary shall manage the literary Competitions held on the occasion of the conference and other literary activities of the Union.

ii. He/ She shall be the 'Editor' of the Mouth-Piece of the Union.

54. The Assistant Literary Secretary.

i. The Assistant Literary Secretary shall manage the literary competition held on the occasion and other literary activities in absence of the literary Secretary.

ii. He/ She shall be the Editor of the Mouth-Piece of the Union in the absence of Literary Secretary.

55. The Sports Secretary.

i) The Sports Secretary shall manage the Games and Sports competition held on the occasion of the Union.

56. The Assistant Sports Secretary.

i) The Assistant Sports Secretary shall help to the Sports Secretary in the maintaining of the Games & Sports competition held on the occasion of the conference and shall also maintain the same in the absence of the Sports Secretary.

57. The Debating Secretary.

i. The Debating Secretary shall manage the Debating competitions held on the occasion of the conference of the Union.

ii. He/ She shall arrange debating competitions from time to time in consultation with the CWC/ABSU.

iii. He/ She shall have the power of selecting the topics of debating competition held at any

time.

58. The Treasurer.

  i. The fees of the members of C.C., ABSU and the CWC/ABSU shall be received by the Treasurer.
 ii. In order to enhance the fund of the Union he/she shall make economic policies, the outcome of such policies shall be in his/her hands.

59. The Educational Secretary.

i) The Educational Secretary shall look after the matters pertaining to all Educational aspects as enshrined in the aims and objectives of the constitution.

60. The Assistant Educational Secretary.

In Absence of the Educational Secretary, the Assistant Educational Secretary shall discharge the duties of the Educational Secretary.

61. The executive members.

  i. All the Executive members shall have the right to speech and vote in the CWC/ABSU and in the meetings of the Sub-Committees for the Conference of the Union.
 ii. One-Tenth members of the CWC/ABSU shall have the power to convene the meeting of the CWC/ABSU when the president, the Secretaries and speakers remain inactive. One Third of the total members of the CWC/ABSU shall make a quorum of the meeting Concerned on such a situation.
iii. Under (ii) above, the member presents shall select a President from among the senior members among themselves for the meeting.
 iv. No member shall have power to deliver to speech beyond collective opinion

62. The office bearers and the executive members of the S.C./D.D.,& A.C./ABSU

i) The power and function of the office bearers and the executive members of the C.C./ABSU incorporated to this Chapter shall also be similarly exercised by those of C.C., S.C.,
D.C. and A.C./ABSU with certain exception as the case may be

CHAPTER-IX

Chapter ix of the constitution of ABSU discuss about the fund and the finance system of the Union:

FUND AND FINANCE

63. The C.C, SCs and ACs/ABSU shall have separate funds of their own.

64. The fund of the CC/ABSU shall the strengthened by collecting donations and subscription from any person and Organization.

   a. Notwithstanding section 14, under emergency circumstances or in normal situation having the due exigency, the central committee/ABSU shall have the power to adopt direct fund collection drive to improve the fund position.
   b. The fund of SC, DC. And A.C/ABSU shall be strengthened through any means suited from them.

65. (i) The delegates' fees receipts in the conference of the C.C./ABSU, SC,/ABSU, D.C/ABSU and A.C/ABSU shall go to their respective funds.

   (ii) The observe fees received in the conference shall go to the reception committee.

66. Separate for magazine shall be created by the collection donation and subscription to each organizational level of ABSU.
67. The fund of the C.C, SC, DC, and A.C/ABSU shall be kept in a PASS BOOK in the name of the treasurer of the respective committee/ABSU.

68. (i) The General Secretary shall present an annual budged in the CWC/ABSU.

(ii) The CWC/ABSU, if necessary shall make change modifications to the budget.

69. (i) There shall be cash balance of 1000/- (One thousand) only with all the General Secretary of a SC/ABSU,DC/ABSU and A.C/ABSU for meeting the emergency expenditure.
70. The General Secretary of the CC, SC, DC, AC,/ABSU shall require the maintain official records such a receipt Books, Cash Books etc. of the respective committee.
71. The accounts of such committee/ABSU shall require to be audited at the end of every year. The auditors shall submit and audit report after the audit.[1]

After discussing the organizational structure of ABSU we can understand that ABSU work in a very organized way according to the provision of the constitution of ABSU. The organization work in a three tire system Central District and Anchalik.

[1]. ABSU, *Constitution of the All Bodo Students Union (as per the English Amendment)*, (Kokrajhar, Narzary printers, 2005), 2-19

BRIEF DISCUSSION ON BODOLAND MOVEMENT

○ : HISTIRICAL PERSPECTIVE OF BODOLAND MOVEMENT

The Bodoland movement has been the most stringent Tribal movement in Assam. This movement has seeded in the colonial times but intensified into a radical political, cultural and extremist assertion in the 1980s the Bodoland Movement draws its sources from the ostensible feeling of discrimination, deprivation and injustice experience by the Bodo Communities in Assam. During the campaign in order to attain political, economic and cultural suzerainty, the leader of the Bodoland movement emphasize that the Bodo people are ethnically different from rest of the people of present day Assam and hence entitled to political entitlement in the form a separate state- Bodoland. This study will try to trace the trajectory in the Bodoland movement from the colonial period to contemporary stage. The various factors which come into play for the intention of the movement, the consolidation process and stage.

WHO ARE THE BODOS?

The Bodos are an ethnic community comprising a number of groups speaking more or less common language and claiming a common ancestry. In the pre-colonial history, they are referred to as Kacharies of Assam. They are believed to have inhibited the fertile plains of the Brahmaputra River in the 12th Century and were pushed away from their original place by the invading Tai- Ahom and Indo- Aryan group to karbi and North Cachar hills in 16th century. Though three is a huge contestation of the exact number of sub-groups under the larger Bodo family. In the present times, they are the largest plain tribes of Assam who inhabit the northern area of the Brahmaputra valley, namely, in places, Kokrajhar, udalguri, chirng, Baksa, Darrang, Sonitpur, Kamrup, Nalbari, Barpeta and Dhubri. The Bodos are found in various North Eastern states like Nagaland, Tripura, Meghalaya and Arunachal Pradesh and also spread acroos international boundaries to Nepal, Bangladesh and Bhutan. Bodo-Kacharis is a branch of the Indo-Mongoloid group falling within the Tibeto-Burmese linguistic section.

Ethnicity and identity have been the key issues of mobilization in all of Northeast India. The movement has its emergence since the colonial period. The issue of land alienation, Marginalization faced from the mainstream and dominant community and the prolonged social and economic backwardness due to the step-motherly treatment of the state has been the main driving factor of the movement. The Bodos thought they claim to be the original inhabitants of the Brahmaputra valley has suffered in the hands of resources, land alienation where a large chuck of land was grabbed from them and also dismal electorate representation in the colonial era. The general feeling of the Bodos is that of neglect, Exploitation, Alienation and decimation for decades.

Structural factors, including economic, social and political issues relating to land and resources, facilitating factors, including the degree of politicization and ethnic consciousness, and triggering factors, such as discriminatory government policies and demographic aggression in to tribal land are concede to be root causes of Bodo conflict in Assam. Moreover, when India attained

her freedom from British Rule in 1947, The Bodos, though they were the original inhabitant of the north east did not get due important in the formation of the geo-political structure of the country.

The various polices adopted by dominant Assamese community post independent has led to the feeling of insecurity threat to their identity by the minority group including Damasas, Karbis, Bodos etc. Further, the Assamese move to make Assam a 'Nation provenance' and the relentless stride towards homogenization and the forceful assertion of identity to the minority has back fired and led to the aggravation of the colonial ethnic cleavage. The introduction of the official language bill on 10th October, 1960 which tries to enforce the use of Assamese as the official language across Assam by the than State government. All these move apart from others has further widened the ethnic cleavage and threatened the linguistic identity of the monitories. The minorities and the Bodos in particular are demanding for self-assertion and determination through the demand for autonomy i.e. for a separate Bodo state, BODOLAND. This move is adopted in the first place since the Bodos who are plain tribes are not covered under 5th and 6th schedule extension in the state of Assam .The Aim and the purpose of this autonomy movement is not only to bring change in the existing system, but also to augment legitimate expression of aspiration by the people having distinct culture, tradition and common patter of living

After going through the historical perspectives of Bodoland movement, we came to know that the Bodoland movement is not emerge out of a vacuum, it is a result of long agitation movement of Bodos. The Bodoland movement seeded in the colonial period but intensified in to a radical political, cultural and extremist assentation in the 1980s.

∘ : CAUSES OF BODOLAND MOVEMENT:

The Bodoland movement did not emerge out of a vacuum. It is a product of a long distinct process of identity formation among the Bodos that started in the colonial period and become assertive in the post-independent period. There are many reasons behind this movement, some of these are mention bellow:

a. Alienation of Tribal land:

Alienation of Tribal land is one of the main cause of Bodoland movement. Land problem is the one of the most burning problem of the tribals of Assam. In fact tribal cannot live without land, without land, lives of common tribal people become very miserable which is now happening to tribal of Assam. Now, about 70% of tribal families have become practically landless whereas 90% of tribal people depend on agriculture. Little plot of agricultural lands cannot suffice the trials to procure a good harvest to cover up whole year for their maintenance of food. As a result, most of the tribal families are half-starved. So Alienation of Tribal land is one of the important cause of

Bodoland movement, as the Bodos society is an agricultural based society, therefore protection of tribal land is very much important but unfortunately the government fails to protect the land of tribals from the encroachment of the non-tribals.

a. Non- Inclusion of Plain Tribes within 6ᵗʰ Schedule:

During the time of farming of the constitution of India, the six Schedule of the constitution was farmed to provide autonomy for the tribels of North-East India. But the plains tribe was mot included under the Six Schedule. Therefore, in the Post-Independent period, the plain tribes demanded for autonomy under the Six Schedule of the Indian Constitution, so the non-inclusion of plain tribes of Assam in to the Six Schedule is also another important cause of Bodoland movement.

c. Problem of illegal migration:

Another important cause of Bodoland movement is the problem of illegal migration to the Bodo dominated area of Assam .Due to the rise of migration in the tribal area of Assam as well as particularly in the BTAD area many problem have been seen in this area. Basically, the problem of job opportunity of the local tribal people, communal conflict and we can also see that most of the tribal land has been illegally occupied by the illegal migrant. So we can also say that the problem of illegal migration is another important cause of Bodoland movement.

d. Growth of organization:

The plain tribes of Assam had their own political platform even in the pre-independent period, the formation of Plain Tribals League in 1933 was the first attempt in this regard. Gradually the Bodo people become educated and conscious about their identity. The sense of identity consciousness was articulated through the various organization. These are-
Assam Bodo Chatra Sanmilan (1918), All Assam Plains Tribal League (1933), Bodo Satiya Sabha (1952) All Bodo Students union (1987)
Plain tribal Council of Assam (1967) Bodo Security force
Bodo Liberation Tiger Force (1993) etc.
All these organization created a sense of self-consciousness about own identity, which led to growth of Bodoland movement.

e. Step-motherly Treatment of Government:

The Assam Government whether the past or present are not the Government of the people of Assam but it is merely a Government of Assamese people particularly the Aaom Gana Parishad Government which had elected to power out of Assam Chauvinism wave. State does not act accordance with the needs of tribal aspiration, so this also can be stated as one of the cause of Bodoland movement.

f. Forceful assimilation policy:

Another cause of Bodoland movement is that of Forceful Assimilation policy of Assamese government, whether it case of language or other aspect of life of the tribal bodos. The chauvinistic attitude of Assamese people is also resopansabioul for the emergence of Bodoland movement.

g. Assamese Chauvinism:

Another most important cause of Bodoland movement is the Assamese Chauvinism. One of the most important responsible factors as why the tribals have become alienated from the mainstream of Assam, is the attitude of the Assamese people. The Assamese people have never accepted the tribals as the part and parcel of Assamese community and society in real sense, though they give a motivated slogan of Greater Assamese Nationality. The real Assamese chauvinistic attitude revel that the greater Assamese Nationality never existed and does not exist even today, so the Assamese Chauvinism is also responsible to the emergence of Bodoland movement.

h. Repressive Government:

The Assam Government and Administration was deadly repressive upon the plains tribals particularly the Bodo Youth and Students. Whenever the plains Tribals demand and cry for justice, constitutional and legitimate rights they are meted out with brutal police atrocities and torture. ON the pretext of forged cases the Assam police forces in tribal areas, arrest the innocent Tribal Youths and Students indiscriminately, Strip them naked and beat up and torture them. The cause is nothing but simply for demanding a Separate State and struggling for preservation of their own identity and culture. So the repressive attitude is also another cause of Bodoland movements.[1]

[1] . P.C Dutta, *Autonomy movement in Assam*,(New Delhi, Omsons Publication, 1993), 271-291

○ : PHASES OF BODOLAND MOVEMENT:

The bodoland movement can be divided in to three phases, these are:

1st Phases (1987-1993):

Under the leadership ABSU a movement for separate state was launched on 2nd March 1987. On that historic day all the Bodo dominated district of Assam held mass Rally proclaiming the demand of a separate state with Upendra Nath Brahma as the leader. Upendara Nath Brahma whom the Bodos call the father of the Bodos or Bodofa, like any other great leaders in the world, had the charismatic personality to infuse the people with revolutionary sprits. This historic proclamation of 2nd March sent massage to the world that the Bodos in Assam had launched a political movement for their own safeguard .On 23 March 1987 the ABSU took out demonstration in front of D.C., S.D.O. and S.D.C. office throughout the state.

Again a historic Mass Rally was organize at Judges Field, Guwahati on 12 June 1987. Thousands of people showed their support to the movement of the ABSU by attending the Mass Rally. The 12 June has gone down in history for the Bodos as an important day, because on that day Sujit Nrzary a student of class x from Batipara, Kokrajhar become martyr at the hands of some chauvinistic Assamese people who were against the Bodos. This incident only added a mental injury to the Bodos who were shouting for justice and rights, and forced them to stir mire vigorously than ever. In the course of Bodoland movement as well as in the lives of the Bodos as of now 12 June has become special day for the reason stated above. This is observed as Martyrs Day. Then again on 2nd June 1987, a demonstration was staged in front of Janata Bhawan, Guwahati. On 21 July 1987 an all Religious Prayer Meeting was held at district level throughout the state. On that same day the Bodos took a vow to keep the struggle on till the achievement of separate state. Again on 10 August 1987 a programme of Hunger Strike was organize in front of the D.C., S.D.O. and S.D.C. offices.

On 10 November 1987 a Mass Demonstration was staged at Boat Club, New Delhi where around 1500 ABSU activists and supporters tool part. A procession from India Gate to Rafi Marg over the Rajpath was also performed on the same day and met the Prime Minister, Rajiv Gandhi and Lok Sabha Speaker, Balaram Jakar and also submitted memorandum to each of them.

A new chapter developed in the movement of the ABSU with the formation of Bodo Peoples Action Committee (BPAC) on 8 November 1988. The 20th Annual Conference of the All Bodo Students Union was held from 18 to 22 December 1988 at Bashbari in Dhubri District. It was in that conference that the separate state demanded by the ABSU was given the nomenclature "BODOLAND". The other important decision of the delegate meeting in the conference was dropping the 89 points of demands related to socio-economic problems out the

original 92 charter of demands. The ABSU decided to focus its attention on the three political demands:

a. Separate state for the Bodos on the northern bank of the Brahamaputra.

b. Creation of Karbi Anglong Regional Council within the District Autonomous Council for the non-Karbi tribal population.
c. Formation of an Autonomous Council for the Bodos on the southern bank of Brahmaputra.

On 14 August 1989 the ABSU and the BPAC declared a 100 hour Assam Bandh, but this bandh was called off as the central govt. for the first time called Tripartite Talk on Bodo Issue in New Delhi. Accordingly a tripartite talk of the center, the state and the representatives of the ABSU-BPAC was held in new Delhi on 28 August 1989.This talk was presided over by Mrs. Rajendra Kumari Bajpayee. The delegation team of the ABSU-BPAC raised the issue of separate state very strongly during the talk. As a result of this talk on 21 October 1990 Union Minister of labor and welfare Mr. Ram Vilas Paswan visited Kokrajhar. More than ten lakh people gathered at the Debargaon field to welcome him as well to show their popular support to the demand of the separate state.

Even after the lapse of the considerable period no response was received from either State or Central government except hollow verbal assurance. The ABSU-BPCA once again declared a 1001 hour Assam bandh starting from 21 November 1992. Large scale violence broke out during this bandh Looking at the grim mood the bandh the then Home Minister Mr. S.B. Chavan called uopon the ABSU-BPAC leaders to put an end to the bandh by giving an assurance that the Government would take measure to solve the Bodoland problem.

With the advent of 1993 talk on Bodoland problem was respond. By then Congress party had come to power at the Centre and Rajesh Pilot, the then State Home Minister, was given charge to look after the Bodo issue. On 20 January 1993 Mr. Pilot had a protracted talk with the president of the ABSU Mr. S.K. Bwiswmuthiary. On 10th February of the same year Mr. Pilot had talk with Hiteswer Saikia, the then Chief Minister of Assam. This talk turn out to be decisive one in bringing about political solution to the Bodoland problem.

The 20th February, 1993 has become another important day in the history of Bodoland movement, because on that the political movement of ABSU-BPAC formally come to an end. An agreement known as Bodo Accord was signed by representatives of central and state Governments on one hand and the ABSU-BPAC on the other. This brought many changes in the political agenda of Bodoland movement. Through this Accord Bodoland Autonomous Council was created. It is noteworthy that the accord was signed in Guwahati, Assam and the signatories were Mr. Rajesh Pilot who represented Central Government, Chif Secretary of Assam, K.S Rao representing state Government and Mr. S.K. Bwiswmuthiary, President and Mr. Rabiram Brahma, Secretary of the ABSU. Mr. Subhas Basumatary, Chairman of the BPAC was also sa signatory of the accord. Both

the state and central government made declaration that with this accord the Bodo issue involving political, economic, linguistic and cultural problems had been resolved. With doubts as well as aspiration the first phase of six years long Bodoland formally came to an end.

2nd phase (1993-2003):

Second phase of Bodoland movemrnt was started again when in 1996 Mr. Garla Bata Baumatari become the president of ABSU in 1993. The problem of demarcation at the autonomous council never ended due to lack sincerity on the part of the Govt. The Central Govt. created touble by setting certain unrespectable condition. It was stated that the strip of land covering ten k.m. from the International Border would not be included in BSE region due to Border Security Reason. Secondly, the reserved forest being a central subject could not be included in BAC area. Thirdly, Sirampur Border get between Assam and Bengal Some Important place such as

Darrang ,Tangla, Etc. Would not be included in the council. It is important to state here that the ground put forward by Govt. for Excluding those areas and place have no constitutional basis. For this reason the boundary Demarcation of the BSE was not drawn till 1996. The lack of political well was frequently compounded by mindless bureaucrats who almost turn the Bodo Accord into a farce. The Bodo Accord signed on 20 February 1993 could have brought a sustainale solution to the Bodo problems for longer period, if it was done in all sincerity.

On 30 July 1996 the extremist its group National democratic Front of Bodoland (NDFB) should that Mr. Swmbla Basumatary, President of ABSU. He was the First President of ABSU to be short that while holding office. Many observed had the opinion that the political turmoil period was responsible for this.

Bodo extremist its Organisation called Bodo Liberation Tigers popularly known as BLT was formed in 1996. Conforming to the political demand if the ABSU, the BLT adopted an ideology of creating a separate state remaining within the Sovereignty of India. Truly speaking, this organization sprang up from the background of the six year Bodoland Mass movement.

After the assassination of Mr.Swmbla Basumatary, Mr,Urkhao Gwra Brahma become the president of ABSU in 1996. In the same year on the occation of the independence day celebration of 15 August the then PM of India H.D. Dev Gowda in his address from Redfort, New Delhi made a statement that Govt. Of India was in favour in creating 3New state namely Jharkhand, Uttarakhand and Chattishgarh the central that the oldest Bodoland demand. ABSU welcome the statement of PM and reminded by the bOdo people should be conceded. Mr. H.D. Dev Gowda visited Assam on 1996. During his visit a delegation team of ABSU made him at Rajbhawan a huge mass rally was organized on Oct'28 1996 at Jugs field Guwahati. In order to transformed the bodoland movement into a mass movement the ABSU in its 30thannual conference held from 1-3 April'1998 at Dudhnoi the Bodo people action committee was broad back to life with Mr. Gobinda Boro and Mr. Reo reoa narzihary as the chairman and the convener respectively the BPAC had a

great role in Bodoland moment without BPAC the ABSU mass moment for Bodoland would have been very difficult. BPAC broad people together and led them to the conviction for separate state.

After the accusation of Swmbla Basumatary till that time there was no solution inside for Bodo issue the birth of the NDFB and BLT was the evidence of this. As NDFB consider All Bodo organization as its enemy's fratricidal killing took place frequently. If we examine the root cause of the conflict within the family we can see the ideology of NDFB as the, main cause of trouble, because the mass people could not support the ideology of sovereignty in the true sense of the term. BLT on the other hand, took the arms struggle to demand a separate state out of Assam but within India. The mass people extended their support to BLT In the interest of ultimate goal the Bodoland State. But the roads of the ABSU and BLT are quite different although there goal is the same. The ABSU and BLT has Difference with regard to democracy, but they have never been hostile to each other in the Second Phase of Bodoland movement, due to extremist groups, several violence took place. The govt. must be held responsible for this to a great extent, as it showed difference or lack of seriousness when people tried to approach it in the democratic way.

The central govt. has no clear policy on this issue. The Assam govt. on the other hand is not ready to cast of its malevolent rigidity it must be mention here that since the month of May'2000 the BLT and the Central Govt. Have been holding talks on Bodoland Issue. All the Bodo organizations are keeping a close eye on tis development.

In the year 2000, the Central Government acknowledged the demands of BLT and invited the leaders for talks and finally on February 10, 2003, an Accord was signed between the leaders of the BLT and Government of India. This Accord pave the way for the formation of the Bodoland Territorial Council under the Sixth Schedule of the Indian Constitution. The New Bodo Accord ushered new phase in the settlement of the Bodo issue. The ABSU leaders extended their support in the talks held between the BLT leaders and the Government. So with the formation of Bodoland Territorial Council the long second phases Bodoland movement came to an end.[2]

3rd Phases (2003 to onward)

Third Phase of Bodoland movement started after the creation of Bodoland Territorial Council on 2003. Though there was a mutual understanding among the leaders of ABSU, Bodo Sahitya Sabha (BSS) and BLT regarding the settlement of Bodo issues. But the creation of BTC also unable to address the grievances as aspirations of the Bodos as a whole. However, in the third phase of Bodoland movement another Bodo militant group was adamant on sovereignty issues and continued their armed struggle. The organization named National Democratic Front of Bodoland

[2] . Yamao Zwhwlao Brahma, Reo Reoa Narzihary, Urkhao Gwra Brahma, Uthrisar Khunggur Basumatary, Damasu Brahma, *Bodoland Movement 1986-2001: a Dream and Reality,9introductory note)* (Kokrajhar, Saraighat Offset Press, 2001) 6-10

(NDFB) is still active carrying out its disruptive activities. Some argued that NDFB has tied with other militant fractions active in the region such as United Liberation Front of Assam, Nationalist Socialist Council of Nagaland, and People's Liberation Army. However over the years, there was a split both ULFA and NDFB. One fraction of ULFA as well as NDFB has announced Ceasefire and come forward for talks. But another fraction is still standing stiff on their demand of sovereignty. Under such circumstances, the prospect of talk still looms in the cloud of uncertainty.

After the creation of Telangana on 2nd June, 2014 All Bodo Student Union (ABSU) said that this time the demand for Bodoland would be "do or die" movement. The ABSU had announced a 12 hour rail blocked on August 2, and 60 hour Assam August 5-7, 2014. The student body was also having a plan of launching a 1000 hours stir.

ABSU President Promod Boro said that "The Initiative taken for creation of Telangana is discriminatory because it has undermined our long movement for separate Bodoland. ABSU has been spearheading the movement for creation of Bodoland for safeguarding the identity of Bodos. But today, we are very much disappointed at the way the government is moving ahead with the formation of Telangana".

Mr. Boro also added that "There is no other way to make our democratic movement more vigorous. This is the right we have as citizens".

People's Action Joint Committee for Bodoland Movement (PJACBM), a conglomeration of 55 outfits of various ethnic groups in the proposed Bodoland, said it is closely monitoring the Congress-led UPA government's move in the creation of Telangana.

Supporting the creation of Telangana, NDFB-P, which has been holding dialogue with the Centre for the last seven years, recently said the creation of Bodoland has become an imperative for safeguarding the identity, culture and protection of lands of the Bodos.

NDFB-P general secretary B Swmkhwr said in New Delhi that, "We want to protect, safeguard and preserve our identity with our language and cultural heritage under the provisions of Constitution so that we can live with dignity and honour. The state government has failed to protect these rights".

So we can say that after the declaration of creation of Telangana by Central Government, it gives a base to the ABSU leader to continue the democratic movement creation of separate state of Bodoland more vigorously. In this third phase of Bodoland movement ABSU have been taking more prominent step and techniques to provide a momentum to the Bodoalnd movement

○ OPPOSATION FROM ASSAMESE COMMUNITY IN BODOLAND MOVEMENT

We cannot deny the fact that there was always an opposition from Assamese community in the separate movement of ABSU, when the Bodos cry out "divide Assam fifty-fifty" it creates a deep impact on the mind of caste Hindu Assamese people. They fear that if fifty percent land is detached from the state of Assam and allowed to form a separate state called Bodoland, Assam would be left to a grave destiny. Infect, C.S Mullanas prophecy that "Sibsagar district will be the only apart of Assam in which an Assamese will find himself at home" Still hunts them. Therefore, the anti-statehood organizations are shouting on the highways and streets that they will rather shed their blood than allow bifurcation of even an inch of Assam land. Even the Assam chief minister Tarun Gogoi, rejecting the division of Assam said, "I am not going to divide Assam. We all need to live together." He further said, "When we are one, others will fear to break us up. We may be Rabhas, Bodos, Chutiyas, Karbis, Gorkhas, Bengalis or minorities. But we all need to live together as Assamese under an umbrella in the state of Assam from Sadiya to Dhubri". The same echo is heard from J.B Patnayak, than governor of Assam when he said, "Assam will not be divided. There is no necessity for separate state as all the ethnic groups can be represented in the Autonomous Council which can take care of the development activities.

Infect, that a section of the Assamese community has been vehemently opposing to granting of geo-political power to the Bodos since the 1980s. They oppose to the creation of Bodoland Autonomous Council and the Bodoland territorial Council. Despite their opposition the governments of

India and Assam granted to the Bodos an Autonomous Council in 1993 and a Territirial Council in 2003 extending Constitutional safeguard under six schedule. Now when the Bodos are once again on their way to agitation for the creation of separate Bodoland State several Assamese organizations have come up to stand against bifurcation of Assam and thereby creation of Bodoland. The attitude of the Assamese people towards the Bodos is one of condemnation only. Any incident that takes place in BTC area or in Assam, the Bodos are be blame. Many intellectuals have alleged that the Bodos are out to make BTC area exclusively for themselves and that is why they are restoring the cleansing of other ethnic groups.[3]

After discussing the historical perspectives of Bodoland movement and going through the possible causes of Bodoland movement, we came to know that Bodoland movement is a result of decimation faced by the bodos from colonial time itself. The Bodoland movement has been the most stringent tribal movement in contemporary Assam, which can also be drscribe as an identity movement. And after discussing the phases of Bodoland movement we came to know that this movement has started in the colonial period and it's still continuing, so probably its one of the most longest Social movement in the history of Assam.

[3] . Hira Charan Narzinary, *The Saga Of Bodos,*

CHAPTER FOUR

ROLE OF ABSU IN BODOLAND MOVEMENT

1. ROLE OF ABSU IN BODOLAND MOVEMENT:

The All Bodo Students Union is the organization of All Bodo Students. It was only after the 1967 that all District and Anchalik Bodo Students Unions are come under the same banner of All Bodo Students Union (ABSU) in the Present form.

While Srimati Indira Gandhi the then Prime minister of India Announced the policy of recognisation of Assam on federal basis before the delegation team of Mizo Union in New Delhi on 13 January 1996. The Goalpara District Bodo Students Union Warmly welcomed the policy and since then demanded a separate state for the plains triblas peoples of Assam. In this away, the ABSU, since its inception till today has been demanding and fighting for a separate state with the status of union territory for the plains tribes of Assam and now for a separate state within the jurisdiction of India.

Reason behind ABSUs movement for separate state:

1. Force homogenization and hegemonic character of chauvinistic Assamese people.
2. Land alienation and excessive enforcement of out siders caused the out number of tribal people in their restricted land which make them feeling insecurity.
3. Economic deprivation and less job opportunities of the Bodos

4. Ignoring the implementation of close of 10 Assam Accord for the benefit of tribal people of Assam.
5. Assamisation policy of Assam Government.

∘ : MAJOR ROLE OF ABSU IN BODOLAND MOVEMENT FORM 1967-

1987:

Movement in 1960s:

While the Assamese people launched a vigorous movement in 1960s for making Assamese language as the soul official language of Assam the Bodo Students and people along with other linguistic minority community launched movement for retention of English as the official language of Assam along with the Assamese-

a. Introduction of Bodo Medium in primary level in 1963.

The Bodo Students Union took the pioneering role and initiative along with the Bodo Sahaitya Sobha in Introducing Bodo Medium in primary level in 1963.

b. Movement in 1968 for Bodo medium of Instruction in secondary stage:

In 1968 Kokrajhar District Bodo Sahitya Sobha and All Bodo Students Union Jointly launched a vigorous movement for recognition of Bodo as a medium of instruction in secondary stage and got the demand fulfilled.

c. Participation in political renaissance of Bodos since 1967:

As stated earlier with the declaration of policy of reorganization of Assam on federal Structure on the 13 January, 1967 the then PM Smt. Indira Gandhi a political Renaissance are among the Bodos and the ABSU took the initiative to form a political party and thus the plains tribal council of Assam (PTCA) Created was on 27 feb'1967 at Kokrajhar. Since then ABSU supported PTCA in demand of a separate State and had been working together for the same Couse. The ABSU withdraw it support to PTCA only in 1977.

Awakening linguistic, socio-culture movement the ABSU had been and still awakening a linguistic literary and socio-cultural movement among the plains tribal and bodos in particular

d. ABSU's role in Bodoland movement in 1972:

The ABSU launched a vigorous movement for retention of English as a medium of instruction in Colleges while the all Assam Students Union launched movement for making Assamese as the soul medium of instruction in colleges in Assam.[1]

e. Participation of ABSU for roman script movement in 1977-1975.

The Bodo Sahatiya Sobha launched a vigorous mass movement in 1974-75 for adoption of roman script for bodo language. The ABSU actively participated in the movement and thousands of ABSU activists had to undergo rigorous misery, arrest and torture during the period of movement. But, unfortunately the demand was not conceded, instead Devanagari Script was imposed to the bodo language.

f. Role of ABSU for political unification:

The ABSU tried its based a unify the split political parties of (Progressive) for launching a concerted movement for separate state but fail due to the adamant and arrogant attitude of the PTC leader.

g. Bodo Associate official language:

The ABSU has tremendous contribution struggling for recognition of bodo as associate official language of Assam in Kokrajhar District and Udalguri sub-Division in 1984.

h. Movement for 92.Chater of Demand ABSU had launched
    movement for the fulfillment of its 92.charter of demand since
    the 2nd March 1987.

¹. P. C Dutta, *Autonomy Movement In Assam(Document)*, *(New Delhi, Omsons Publication, 1993)*, *259-261*

∘ : ROLE OF ABSU IN BODOLAND MOVEMENT SINCE 1987:

- ABSU, under the leadership Upendra Nath Brahma started a movement for separate state was on 2nd March 1987. On that historic day all the Bodo dominated district of Assam held mass Rally proclaiming the demand of a separate state. Upendara Nath Brahma whom the Bodos call the father of the Bodos or Bodofa, like any other great leaders in the world, had the charismatic personality to infuse the people with revolutionary sprits. This historic proclamation of 2nd March sent massage to the world that the Bodos in Assam had launched a political movement for their own safeguard .On 23 March 1987 the ABSU took out demonstration in front of D.C., S.D.O. and S.D.C. office throughout the state.

- Again a historic Mass Rally was organize at Judges Field, Guwahati on 12 June 1987. Thousands of people showed their support to the movement of the ABSU by attending the Mass Rally. The 12 June has gone down in history for the Bodos as an important day, because on that day Sujit Nrzary a student of class x from Batipara, Kokrajhar become martyr at the hands of some chauvinistic Assamese people who were against the Bodos. This incident only added a mental injury to the Bodos who were shouting for justice and rights, and forced them to stir mire vigorously than ever. In the course of Bodoland movement as well as in the lives of the Bodos as of now 12 June has become special day for the reason stated above. This is observed as Martyrs Day.

- Then again on 2nd June 1987, a demonstration was staged in front of Janata Bhawan, Guwahati. On 21 July 1987 an all Religious Prayer Meeting was held at district level throughout the state. On that same day the Bodos took a vow to keep the struggle on till the achievement of separate state. Again on 10 August 1987 a programme of Hunger Strike was organize in front of the D.C., S.D.O. and S.D.C. offices.

- On 10 November 1987 a Mass Demonstration was staged at Boat Club, New Delhi where around 1500 ABSU activists and supporters tool part.

A procession from India Gate to Rafi Marg over the Rajpath was also performed on the same day and met the Prime Minister, Rajiv Gandhi and Lok Sabha Speaker, Balaram Jakar and also submitted memorandum to each of them.

- Another role of ABSU is that form a committee namely, Bodo Peoples Action Committee (BPAC) on 8 November 1988. The 20th Annual Conference of the All Bodo Students Union was held from 18 to 22 December 1988 at Bashbari in Dhubri District. It was in that conference that the separate state demanded by the ABSU was given the nomenclature "BODOLAND".
- ABSU in its 20th conference dropped the 89 points of demands related to socio-economic problems out the original 92 charter of demands. The ABSU decided to focus its attention on the three political demands:

    a. Separate state for the Bodos on the northern bank of the Brahamaputra.
    b. Creation of Karbi Anglong Regional Council within the District Autonomous Council for the non-Karbi tribal population.

    c. Formation of an Autonomous Council for the Bodos on the southern bank of Brahmaputra.

- On 14 August 1989 the ABSU and the BPAC declared a 100 hour Assam Bandh, but this bandh was called off as the central govt. for the first time called Tripartite Talk on Bodo Issue in New Delhi. Accordingly a tripartite talk of the center, the state and the representatives of the ABSU-BPAC was held in new Delhi on 28 August 1989.This talk was presided over by Mrs. Rajendra Kumari Bajpayee. The delegation team of the ABSU- BPAC raised the issue of separate state very strongly during the talk. As a result of this talk on 21 October 1990 Union Minister of labor and welfare Mr. Ram Vilas Paswan visited Kokrajhar. More than ten lakh people gathered at the Debargaon field to welcome him as well to show their popular support to the demand of the separate state.
- Even after the lapse of the considerable period no response was received from either State or Central government except hollow verbal assurance. The ABSU-BPCA once again declared a 1001 hour Assam bandh starting from 21 November 1992. Large scale violence broke out during this bandh Looking at the grim mood the bandh the then Home Minister Mr.

S.B. Chavan called uopon the ABSU-BPAC leaders to put an end to the bandh by giving an assurance that the Government would take measure to solve the Bodoland problem.

- With the advent of 1993 talk on Bodoland problem was respond. By then Congress party had come to power at the Centre and Rajesh Pilot, the then State Home Minister, was given charge to look after the Bodo issue. On 20 January 1993 Mr. Pilot had a protracted talk with the president of the ABSU Mr. S.K. Bwiswmuthiary. On 10th February of the same year Mr. Pilot had talk with Hiteswer Saikia, the then Chief Minister of Assam. This talk turn out to be decisive one in bringing about political solution to the Bodoland problem.

- Another role of ABSU is that ABSU able to influence the government and as a result of that an agreement known as Bodo Accord was signed by representatives of central and state Governments on one hand and the ABSU-BPAC on the other. Through this Accord Bodoland Autonomous Council was created. It is noteworthy that the accord was signed in Guwahati, Assam and the signatories were Mr. Rajesh Pilot who represented Central Government, Chie Secretary of Assam, K.S Rao representing state Government and Mr.

S.K. Bwiswmuthiary, President and Mr. Rabiram Brahma, Secretary of the ABSU. Mr. Subhas Basumatary, Chairman of the BPAC was also a signatory of the accord. Both the state and central government made declaration that with this accord the Bodo issue involving political, economic, linguistic and cultural problems will be solved.

- ABSU played important role when in 1996 Mr. Garla Bata Baumatari become the president of ABSU in 1993. The problem of demarcation at the autonomous council never ended due to lack sincerity on the part of the Govt. The Central Govt. created trouble by setting certain un expectable condition. It was stated that the strip of land covering ten k.m. from the International Border would not be included in BSE region due to Border Security Reason. Secondly, the reserved forest being a central subject could not be included in BAC area.

Thirdly, Sirampur Border get between Assam and Bengal Some Important place such as Darrang ,Tangla, Etc. Would not be included in the council. It is important to state here that the ground put forward by Govt.

for Excluding those areas and place have no constitutional basis. For this reason the boundary Demarcation of the BSE was not drawn till 1996. The lack of political well was frequently compounded by mindless bureaucrats who almost turn the Bodo Accord into a farce. The Bodo Accord signed on 20 February 1993 could not brought a sustainable solution to the Bodo problems for longer period, ABSU protest it.

- Another role of ABSU is that ABSU organize a huge mass rally on Oct, 28 1996 at Jugs field Guwahati. In order to transformed the bodoland movement into a mass movement when Mr. H.D. Dev Goada visited Assam. During his visit a delegation team made him at Rajbhawan.
- The ABSU in its 30th annual conference held from 1-3 April'1998 at Dudhnoi the Bodo people action committee was broad back to life with Mr. Gobinda Boro and Mr. Reo Reoa Narzihary as the chairman and the convener respectively the BPAC had a great role in Bodoland moment without BPAC the ABSU mass moment for Bodoland would have been very difficult. BPAC broad people together and led them to the conviction for separate state.
- On 10 Nov'1987 a mass demonstration was staged at boat club, New Delhi where around 1500 ABSU activists took part and submitted a memorandum to the PM Rajib Gandhi.
- Several time ABSU called for Assam bandh, Rail rook and several other demonstration program, On Feb'22 to 26 May'1988 ABSU called for hundred hour rail roko program, then on 1 to 5 March'1988 ABSU called for highway blocked program, then again on 28 Aprl'1988 a peace rally was held on highway. Son 14 Aug'1989 ABSU called for a hundred hours Assam bandh then again on 1990 to 12 Nov' ABSU called One thousand One Hour Total Assam Bandh.
- Another role of ABSU is that ABSU as student's organization maintained close relation with other student organization of the North East. It participated in the first conference of North Eastern indigenous Students Federation held at Shillong in September 1986. The ABSU includes various Bodo student union of Assam, Meghalaya, West Bengal and Nepal. It also maintains a close relation with the student union of Tripura, Mongolian student organization of the world. ABSU for its well organizational capacity always able to work according to the needs of the Bodos.

- Another role of ABSU is that in addition to political demands, ABSU has demanded solution of all the problems faced by the people. It has demanded fertilizers at subsidized rate to the farmers, water supply, housing, irrigation facilities, flood control, roads and bridges in tribal dominated areas from the state government. It has opposed the decision of AGP government for eviction of tribal settler from reserved and government land. It has also demanded deletion of clause 10 of the Assam accord.

- ABSU has also raise its voice against inhuman treatment meted out to the students and tribal youths by the police. The intense desire and the indomitable spirit of mankind for its survival cannot be suppressed by the police.
- Another role of ABSU in Bodoland movement is that it has formed the Bodo Peoples Action Committee (BPAC) with the help of the people. The committee has wide range of activities.[2]

ROLE OF ABSU IN BODOLAND MOVEMENT: AN OVER VIEW ON CONTEMPORARY ROLE:

ABSU played a supportive role with Bodo Sahitya Sabha to include the Bodo language into the 8th Schedule to the constitution of India, after the signing of the new historic Bodo Accord 2003 it provides for inclusion of Bodo into the 8th Schedule to the Constitution of India. After that the Sahitya Academy initiates for enhance its status and prestige of Bodo language to a great extent. The Indian Public Service Commission also has considered the Bodo language as one of the subject language for their conduct of civil service examinations since 2005.

Another role of ABSU is that ABSU take 2006 as a 'Year of Education' and under this mission ABSU has been doing numbers of educational activities, such as

1. Visiting school/collage to assess the quality education.
2. Taking care about distribution of textbooks in a right time by government official to the students.
3. Put pressure to the government to provide sufficient teachers in the needed Bodo medium school and department of the collages.

4. Encourage to read the Bodo children to their vernacular language (Bodo language) to conserve their language and literature.
5. Conduct educational awareness program in remote and backward places of Bodo populated areas.
6. Special coaching center for different level of School students.
7. Arrangement of orientation program/ special coaching for competitive exam.
8. Arrangement of carrier concealing program for job opportunities.

In the year of 2007 ABSU has taken "Mission Quality Education 20-20". Under this mission ABSU has taken some of these vision

- No Fail

2. Yamao Zwhwlao Brahma, Reo Reoa Narzihary, Urkhao Gwra Brahma, Uthrisar Khunggur Basumatary, Damasu Brahma, *Bodoland Movement 1986-2001: a Dream and Reality,9introductory note)* (Kokrajhar, Saraighat Offset Press, 2001) 6-10

    - My Education My Future
    - Motivational carrier concealing

Another role of ABSU in Bodoland movement in that ABSU always try to bring the social awareness among in Bodo society. ABSU has been taking several steps to abolished evil practice from the Bodo society.

- ABSU have been arranging awareness program to avoid superstation and to stop witch hunting. Witch hunting is an evil practice of Bodo society, along with those ABSU have been taking steps to stop drugs abuse and human trafficking, gambling and polygamy from Bodo society. So here we can say that ABSU is not only concerned about political emancipation among the Bodos, but also playing satisfactory role to remove the social evil practice from Bodo society.

Another role of ABSU in Bodoland movement is that in 2010 ABSU have taken a mission call 'Mission Bodoland' according to this mission ABSU have taken 2019 as a target year to achieve separate state called Bodoland.

At last we can say that during the last three-four year ABSU has been doing lots for the community. However, it is not possible to recall all of them. It has submitted several memorandum to the President of India, Prime Minister and Home minister and discuss with them again and again. ABSU has also discussed with the Assam government but no satisfactory result came out of these discussion, at least ABSU said that they will struggle till their demand came to true.

we came to know that Tribal land alienation is one of the main cause of Bodoland movement. Tribal Land Alienation is the main cause of Bodoland movement, the government fails to protect the lands of tribal and subsequently the tribes feels insecure in their own land and ultimately this led to the emergence of Bodoland movement. Tribal cannot live without land, without land, lives of the common tribal become very miserable which is now happening to the tribals of Assam.

We can see that Economic deprivation is one of the main cause of Bodoland movement. the fact that the indigenes people have been economically deprived since the colonial period to till now is one of the most relevant cause of Bodoland movement initiated by ABSU. The indigenes Bodos have been facing a relative deprivation in the economic aspect and it's a strain to the main Bodos and this fact led to emergence of Bodoland movement.

We found that the step motherly treatment of the government whether central or state government is also one of main responsible cause of Bodoland movement. The government attitudes towards the local Bodos was always a secondary. Government always fails to redress the reverences of aspiration of Bodos and ultimately it led to the emergence of Bodoland movement and ABSU always demand for the equal attenuation to the grievances of the Bodos.

We can see that forceful Assimilation policy is one of the dominant cause of Bodoland movement. Bodos have always feels insecure for the hegemonic and forceful assimilation policies of the Government and ABSU consider it as threat to the identities of Bodos, and subsequently it led to the emergence of Bodoland movement.

We found that Assamese chauvinism is a one of the cause of Bodoland movement. Assamese chauvinism such as linguistic hegemony, forceful assimilation policy are the main cause behind the Bodo movement. Bodos always fight to recognize their language.

ABSU to a great extend become successful to protect the identities of Bodos. ABSU fight to recognize the Bodo language as official language and certain extend ABSU become successful to save the political identities of Bods by the separate state movement. As a result of movement of ABSU now bodos enjoy a save political position in the politics of BTC, Assam and India.

ABSU has been able to provide sound leadership to the Bodoland movement. Leader like Upendra Nath Brahma, whom Bodos consider as the father of Bodos, than the present leader of ABSU Mr. Pramod Boro are the some of the most successful leader of Bodoland movement, it is their leadership, skill and knowledge which make the movement successful till now.

ABSU has been able to materialize the Bodoland movement. It's the ABSU which playing a dominant role in the movement and has been able to materialized the movement to a great extend. Yes ABSU has been able to mobilize the Bodo people for their separate state movement, ABSU with their various awareness programme create a sense of political awareness among the Bodos and successfully able to mobilize the Bodos for the Bodoland movement.

ABSU is the one of the organization of Bodos, which have been taking a leading role in the Bodoland movement. ABSU with other organization of Bodos such as Bodo Sahitya sabha, Bodo people Action Committee and other organization taking a leading role in the Bodoland movement. So from hare we can say that yes ABSU is playing a very important role in Bodoland movement.

ABSU as a Students organization have been able to create a socio-economic and political awareness among the Bodos, ABSU regularly organized several socio-economic and political awareness program, regularly visit school organized several concealing pregame and workshop for the needy. In this way ABSU has been able to create a sense of socio-economic and political awareness among the Bodos.

The movement for separate state of ABSU is an non-violent movement. All tetanic of movement of ABSU such as Hartal, Demonstration, Rally etc. are some of the tactics of non-violent movement, so from hare we can say that the present Bodoland movement of ABSU is a non-violent movement.

ABSU as a Students organization has been able to preserve the rice cultural heritage of Bodos to a great extent. ABSU request the Bodo girls to wear Bodo cultural dress (Dokhona). They campaign to maintain the tribal way of life to the Bodos. ABSU organize cultural rally time to time to showcase the rice cultural heritage of Bodos.

ABSU taking the above mention steps in their movement for separate state. All of these steps are consider as the method of non -violent movement. Some of the steps that ABSU has been taking in their movement are demonstration, railway and highway blocked, hartal, hunger strike and cultural rally.

Bodos are satisfied with the movement of ABSU for separate state. And they are also view that they are satisfied in the movement of ABSU and they believe in due courses of time they will be successful to fulfil their demand for a separate state.

After discussing all the above found data in this research we came to a conclusion that ABSU as non-political and student organization is playing a very satisfactory role in the bodoland movement. ABSU within their several initiative has been able to create a sense of socio-economic and political awareness among the Bodos. We also found that ABSU which have been taking a leading role in the Bodoland movement and has been able to satisfied the Bodos with their movement for separate state. So at least we can say that to a great extent ABSU has been able to protect the identities of Bodos through their Bodoland movement.

CHAPTER FIVE

Conclusion

The Bodoland movement is one of the most prevalent identity movement in Assam and ABSU as a student union playing a very important to materialize the movement.

following are some of the main causes of Bodoland movement.

1. Force homogenization and hegemonic character of chauvinistic Assamese people.
2. Land alienation and excessive enforcement of out siders caused the out number of tribal people in their restricted land which make them feeling insecurity.
3. Economic deprivation and less job opportunities of the Bodos
4. Ignoring the implementation of close of 10 Assam Accord for the benefit of tribal people of Assam.
5. Step-motherly Treatment of Government. Following are the main findings of this study

1. ABSU has been able to mobilize the Bodo people for Bodoland movement.
2. ABSU has been able to materialize the Bodoland movement to a great extent.
3. The movement for the separate state of ABSU is a non-violent movement.
4. ABSU has been able to preserve the rich cultural heritage of Bodos through their separate state movement.
5. ABSU has become successful in protecting the identity of Bodos trough their separate state movement.
6. ABSU has been able to provide sound leadership to the movement.
7. Following are the steps taken by ABSU in Bodoland movement.

- Demonstration
- Hartal
- Hunger strike
- Cultural rally
- Railway and highway blockade

Following are the some of the findings regarding the role of ABSU to abolish the evil practice from the Bodo society.

1. Time to time arranged the awareness program to avoid superstition.
2. Arranged the awareness program to stop witch hunting.
3. Taking step to stop human trafficking.
4. Taking step to stop gambling.
5. Taking step to stop polygamy.

he Bodo issue is yet to come to final settlement, The Bodo movement is one of the longest social movement in the plains of Assam. ABSU a non-political student's organization has a strong voice in this movement for a separate state. However , after the last BTC Accord, these voices of ABSU was lowered down but when Central government declared for a creation of new state call telengana in 2014, ABSU leaders support this step of the government and started a vigorous movement for separate state. So we can say the long Bodoland movement of ABSU got momentum after the creation of telengana in 2014. ABSU is one of the main actor behind the Bodoland movement, since 1987 to till now ABSU playing a very significant role in the Bodoland movement. The main motive of the Bodoland movement of ABSU is to create a separate state call BODOLAND and protect the distinct socio- economic and cultural identities of Bodos. In this long Bodoland movement ABSU have taken so many initiative to mobilize the Bodos for the movement at the same time ABSU has been able to create a socio-economic and politics awareness among the Bodos through their various initiative. At last we can say that so far the movement is going on ABSU has been able to protect the identities of Bodos to a greater extend.

Bibliography:-

1. *Dutta, P.S*, 1993 "Autonomy movement in Assam" (document), Omsons Publications, New Delhi.
2. *Baruah, Sanjib,* 1999, "Assam against itself: assam and politics of nationality", oxford University Press, New Work.
3. *Sen Chaudhuri, Sucheta,* "the Bodo movement and women's participation", A Mittal publication, 2004
4. *Benarjee, A Chandra and Roy, Singh, Sourabh,* 2010, "problems and prospects of Bodoland", Mittal publications, New Delhi (India)
5. *Sonowal, Khema,* 2013, "why bodo movement ?", Pp- 51-55 EBH publication (India) Guwahati 1
6. *Pathak, Jyotiraj,* 2014 "tribal welfare in India" with special reference to North East india, Pp- 96-100, Global publishing House, visakhapatanam, India,
7. *Choudhury, Topu,* 2015, "Bodoland movement: A study", Scholars Publications, Karimganj, Assam.
8. *Pathak, jyotiraj,* "JONER", 2017, Global publishing House, visakhapatanam, India.